AGE OF THE DINOSAUR

Published by the Natural History Museum

Welcome to the
Age of the Dinosaur

Long, long ago there were no tigers or lions, no elephants or giraffes, no seals or whales, and no people. But there were – dinosaurs! From about 230 million years ago, these great beasts ruled the Earth. We call their time the Age of the Dinosaur.

Record-breakers

Different kinds of dinosaurs were among the biggest, fastest and fiercest of all land animals. They lived almost everywhere, from high mountains to forests, deserts and seashores.

➡ Speedy *Ornithomimus* (orn-ITH-oh-MEE-mus) was one of the fastest dinosaurs, able to race along at over 60 kilometres per hour like a racehorse.

Going, gone

No kinds of living things last for ever. The Age of the Dinosaur ended 65 million years ago. Which is perhaps just as well Otherwise you might not be here to read about it!

🐾 Leaf-munching *Iguanodon* (ig-WHA-noh-don) was one of the most common big dinosaurs, as big as an elephant. It left many hundreds of fossils.

🐾 Flesh-chomping *Tyrannosaurus* (tie-RAN-oh-sore-us) was one of the biggest meat-eating dinosaurs, more than 12 metres long.

The best age!

Planet Earth formed over 4,500 million years ago. The first living things were tiny specks in the sea 1,000 million years later. Gradually living things became bigger and more complicated, and spread onto the land.

Not all dinosaurs

Over millions of years many big animals have roamed the land, swam in water and flown in the air. But not all of them were dinosaurs. Some were other kinds of reptiles, and some were not reptiles at all, but mammals, amphibians and birds.

Dimetrodon (die-MEET-roe-don) lived 270 million years ago, before the Age of the Dinosaur. Its tall sail of skin on its back, held up by bony spines, soaked up the sun's heat so it could become active quickly.

Nothosaurs (NO-thow-SORES) lived 220 million years ago, early in the Age of the Dinosaur. They were reptiles but not dinosaurs. They swam in the sea and ate fish and other water creatures.

251
million
years

200
million
years

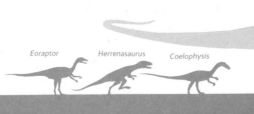

Diplodocus

Camarasaurus

Stegosaurus

Eoraptor   *Herrenasaurus*   *Coelophysis*

Scelidosaurus   *Compsognathus*

Triassic

Jurassic

Mesozoic Era

Dinosaurs lived only during a time called the Mesozoic Era. This had three parts called Periods.

• Triassic Period, 251-200 million years ago. The first dinosaurs were small, but larger ones soon spread around the world.

• Jurassic Period, 200 to 145 million years ago. Some of the biggest dinosaurs lived then, and also some of the tiniest.

• Cretaceous Period, 145-65 million years ago. At its end, all remaining dinosaurs died out.

Dimorphodon (die-MORE-foe-don) lived 195 million years ago, during the Age of the Dinosaur. It was a type of flying reptile called a pterosaur.

Woolly mammoths lived less than one million years ago, long after the Age of the Dinosaur. They were mammals with long fur to keep out the Ice Age cold.

Different kinds of dinosaurs lived all through the Mesozoic Era. There were many other creatures too, like flying pterosaurs and furry mammals.

145 million years

65 million years

Megalosaurus

Archaeopteryx

Iguanodon

Tarbosaurus

Titanosaurus

Baryonyx

Gallimimus

Oviraptor

Lambeosaurus

Tyrannosaurus

Velociraptor

Cretaceous

All about fossils

How can we go back in time to find out about dinosaurs? We study their fossils. These are their bones, teeth, horns, claws as well as their footprints and eggs. They got buried and, over millions of years, turned to stone.

Not just dinosaurs

◀ This fossil from the Jurassic Period shows that starfish over 150 million years ago were very similar to starfish today.

It wasn't only dinosaurs that left fossils. Many other animals did, like fish, snakes, spiders and starfish. So did plants like ferns and trees. Lots of different fossils found in one place show how creatures and plants lived together long ago.

🐾 A fish died. Its soft parts were eaten or rotted away.

🐾 The hard parts like bones and teeth were buried by grains of sand or mud, called sediments.

🐾 The hard parts were buried deeper. Over millions of years they and the sediments turn to stone.

🐾 The hard parts are now fossils. Weather, earthquakes and other forces wear away the rock above to reveal the fossil.

Finding fossils takes care, practice and patience. It is often hard work in difficult conditions such as hot sun or cold winds. These scientists are digging up dinosaur remains in South Africa.

Word search

Find five parts of animals that are often preserved as fossils.

B T X W A L C
M F E Y L N W
B O N E V R J
P K H L T O D
J S H R S H Z

Finding fossils

Experts search for the kinds of rocks that contain fossils, such as limestone and sandstone. These formed mostly on the bottoms of rivers, lakes and seas, trapping and preserving the remains of animals and plants.

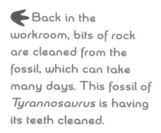

Back in the workroom, bits of rock are cleaned from the fossil, which can take many days. This fossil of *Tyrannosaurus* is having its teeth cleaned.

Dawn of the dinosaurs

The Age of the Dinosaur began over 230 million years ago during the Triassic Period. The world was very different then. All the main land masses, called continents, were joined together into one giant continent called Pangaea (pan-GEE-ah).

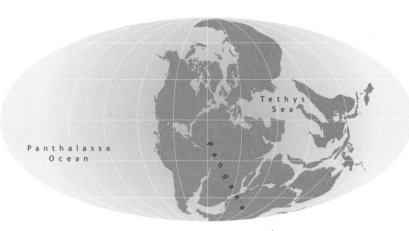

Panthalassa Ocean

Tethys Sea

Pangaea

▼ During the Triassic, Pangaea was made from all the continents joined together.

What was it like?

The edges or coasts of Pangaea were warm, often with plenty of rain. Away from the sea, far inland, it was hot in summer, cold in winter, and dry for most of the year. There were huge deserts and areas of dry scrubland..

▲ During the Triassic Period many parts of the world looked like the deserts of Arizona, USA, with spiky bushes and sandstone rocks.

Early dinosaurs

The first dinosaurs included small meat-eaters such as *Herrerasaurus* (herr-ray-rah-SORE-us). They ran on two back legs. Next came big plant-eaters like *Plateosaurus* (PLAT-ee-oh-SORE-us).

Sharp-toothed *Herrerasaurus* lived about 228 million years ago in South America. At 3 metres it was as long as a lion.

Plateosaurus was one of the first big dinosaurs, up to 10 metres long. Its many teeth were sharp-edged to cut up plant food.

As time went on into the Jurassic, there were more different types of dinosaurs like this *Scelidosaurus* (skel-EYE-doh-sore-us). It was one of the first dinosaurs with hard plates of bone in its skin for protection.

Teeming seas

As dinosaurs spread across the land during the Jurassic, they may have waded or swum to escape enemies. But no dinosaurs lived in the water. However, there were many other kinds of creatures living in Jurassic seas and oceans.

On the sea bed

Many animals in the sea had already been around for millions of years. There were sponges that looked like squishy lumps, and tiny coral creatures that built huge rocky reefs. Starfish crawled across the rocks. Their cousins the sea-lilies waved their long feathery arms to gather tiny bits of food from the water.

Fossils of sea-lilies show how these simple animals lived on the sea bed and attached themselves to driftwood in Jurassic times.

Ammonite shells formed millions of beautiful fossils. When alive, this animal had a head with eyes and tentacles poking out of the shell's wide end.

Sea-lilies, or crinoids, are still common in the sea today. They pass bits of food along the feeding arms to the mouth in the middle.

Shells, eyes and arms

Many kinds of shellfish lived in Jurassic seas, such as mussels, oysters and lampshells. There were also curly-shelled ammonites and straight-bodied belemnites. These fierce hunters had big eyes and bendy arms to grab animals as food.

➤ Jurassic lampshells, also called brachiopods, were almost the same as these lampshells in the sea today.

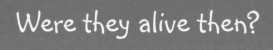

Were they alive then?

Tick which of these sea-dwellers were around during the Jurassic Period?

Starfish ☐

Whales ☐

Sharks ☐

Seals ☐

Sea-lilies ☐

Ammonites ☐

➤ The biggest belemnites were 3 metres long. Like ammonites, they ate fish and any other prey they could catch. They had a long, pointed shell in the rear of the body which is a common fossil.

➤ The fossils of belemnite shells are called 'belemnite bullets'. There are thousands in some rocks, showing how common these creatures were during the Age of the Dinosaur.

Sea-going giants

The Jurassic Period continued, and the world became warmer. More new creatures appeared, including bigger dinosaurs on land. In the sea, some of their reptile relatives were true giants!

Some pliosaurs like *Liopleurodon* (lie-oh-plur-OH-don) were over 10 metres long. They were the biggest hunters of Jurassic seas.

Long necks

Reptiles called plesiosaurs had a very long bendy neck, a tubby body, four flippers and a short tail. They grabbed small prey such as fish and belemnites with their many sharp teeth.

Plesiosaurus (pleez-ee-oh-SORE-us) grew up to 5 metres long. About half of this was its amazing neck!

Big head

Pliosaurs were cousins of plesiosaurs. They had broad, fat bodies with flippers for paddling, but a short neck and huge head.

Today's beaked whales probably live and hunt like pliosaurs did in the Jurassic ocean.

Big teeth

Pliosaurs were the top predators in the Jurassic seas and probably fed on other marine reptiles. They had strong jaws and teeth with sharp cutting edges.

➤ This conical curved fossil pliosaur tooth is as long as a pencil.

Fishy fins

Some Jurassic fish were as small as your hand. Others grew bigger than cars, but they started their lives small too. These little fish were the main food for larger sea hunters.

➤ The Jurassic fish *Dapedium* (dap-ED-ee-um) was up to 40 centimetres long. It had strong scales for protection and a large tail to twist, turn and escape from predators such as plesiosaurs and pliosaurs.

Sea monsters

The world's continents were drifting apart during the Jurassic. There were many warm shallow seas called lagoons. In them swam some real sea monsters!

Fast fish-eaters

Among the fastest swimmers were ichthyosaurs. They had long, slim jaws with sharp teeth to catch fish, and upright tails. Like all other reptiles, they did not have gills to breathe underwater. They had to come to the surface to breathe air.

During the Jurassic, lagoons formed as North and South America moved away from Europe and Africa. These lagoons became the Atlantic Ocean.

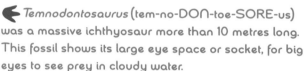
Temnodontosaurus (tem-no-DON-toe-SORE-us) was a massive ichthyosaur more than 10 metres long. This fossil shows its large eye space or socket, for big eyes to see prey in cloudy water.

Ichthyosaurus (ick-THEE-oh-SORE-us) was a small ichthyosaur about 2 metres long. It had a back fin like a shark and also four flippers.

🦶 Sharks swam in the oceans 200 million years before the Age of the Dinosaur. *Hybodus* (hi-BODE-us) had a strong spine in front of each back fin for protection. Like all fish it could breathe underwater using its gills.

Crocodiles

Another group of reptiles that took to living in or near water in Jurassic times were crocodiles. They swam by swishing their long, tapering tails. They probably fed by catching fish or biting lumps out of dead or dying animals.

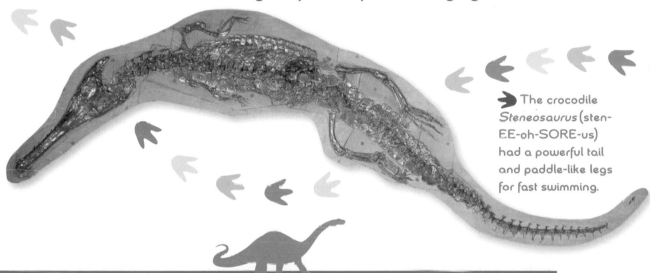

➜ The crocodile *Steneosaurus* (sten-EE-oh-SORE-us) had a powerful tail and paddle-like legs for fast swimming.

Which is which?

Some sea animals had similar shapes for fast swimming. But they were very different creatures. Here are an ichthyosaur, a shark, a Jurassic crocodile and a dolphin. Which is which?

Dinosaur heyday

Life on land during the Jurassic was very different from today. Most places were warm and damp, with huge forests of giant ferns and conifer trees. This is where dinosaurs lived, hunted, escaped enemies, laid eggs, and either survived or died.

Mega-dinosaurs

The giant dinosaurs of 150 million years ago were called sauropods. They were among the biggest animals ever to walk the Earth. They were plant-eaters, swallowing vast amounts of leaves and stems from huge tree-ferns and trees such as conifers and ginkgoes.

Stomach stones

Fossils of sauropods are often found with smoothly rounded stones bigger than your fist. Probably the dinosaurs swallowed these stones into their stomach, to help grind up their tough plant food.

> Sauropod dinosaurs had long necks to swing their heads around and reach lots of food. The biggest Jurassic sauropod was *Brachiosaurus* (brack-EE-oh-SORE-us). It was three times taller than a giraffe!

Mini-dinosaurs

The small dinosaurs were slim and speedy. They could run away from enemies and hide easily. One of the smallest was *Compsognathus* (komp-sog-NATH-us), hardly larger than a pet cat.

◀ *Compsognathus* had long back legs for fast running, a long tail to help it turn quickly, and many sharp teeth to grab small creatures such as flies, dragonflies and beetles.

▲ Only two fossils of *Compsognathus* have been found, one in Germany and one in France. In this fossil the neck is bent back so the head is over the hips and back legs.

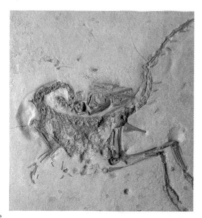

Growing up

Some dinosaurs were even smaller than *Compsognathus*, but they were babies just hatched from eggs. Babies of the plant-eating *Maiasaura* (my-ah-SORE-ah) were just 30 centimetres long, but they grew up to be 9 metres long!

Dinosaurs take off

As the Jurassic moved into the Cretaceous Period, new kinds of creatures took to the skies – birds. Where did they come from, and were they expert fliers or clumsy gliders?

Evolution

Animals and plants change gradually over time, which is known as evolution. Some small meat-eating dinosaurs also evolved into a new kind of creature. They grew long light feathers, their front legs changed shape into wings, and they flew into the air as birds.

Small dinosaurs with feathers escaped enemies by climbing trees, flapping their wings and gliding a short way. Over a long time their arms grew bigger and stronger and dinosaurs became birds.

Feathered dinosaurs

Fossils show that several kinds of small meat-eating dinosaurs grew feathers. However their arms were not strong enough for flight. One reason for feathers in non-fliers might have been to keep warm.

→ The tiny dinosaur *Microraptor* (MIKE-row-rap-tor) had long feathers on its arms, body and legs too, so they were able to glide or flap their wings.

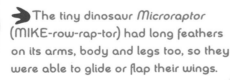

Fossils of the dog-sized dinosaur *Dilong* (DIE-long) show it had fluffy feathers, perhaps to keep in body warmth during cold weather.

Archaeopteryx

The first known bird was *Archaeopteryx* (ark-EE-op-TER-ix). It had teeth in its mouth, claws on its front legs, and long bones in its tail, just like a small meat-eating dinosaur. As birds evolved more, they lost these dinosaur features.

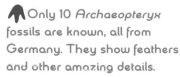 *Archaeopteryx* was probably a good tree-climber and runner. It may have been a good glider too, but not an expert flier like today's birds.

 Only 10 *Archaeopteryx* fossils are known, all from Germany. They show feathers and other amazing details.

Crazy colours!

No one knows the real colours of *Archaeopteryx* or other fossil creatures. Their fossils are the colours of the rocks they are made from. So you can go crazy with this *Archaeopteryx* and use as many colours as you wish!

Busy skies

As the first birds swooped through Late Jurassic and Early Cretaceous skies, they were not alone. There were already many kinds of flying creatures called pterosaurs. Like the dinosaurs below, the pterosaurs were reptiles.

Anurognathus (an-your-oh-NAY-thus) was a very small pterosaur, with a tiny body but with a wing span of two adult hands.

Expert fliers

Pterosaurs were flying reptiles with strong arm muscles to flap their wings and fly well The wings were made of thin skin held out by finger bones, mainly the very long fourth finger. They had sharp claws on their wings and on their feet too.

This fossil skull of *Dimorphodon* shows its large mouth and the big space for its eye. The skull is about 20 centimetres long.

Dimorphodon

Fossils of the pterosaur *Dimorphodon* (die-MORE-foe-don) were first found in Southern England almost 200 years ago, along a stretch of shore with so many fossils it is called the 'Jurassic Coast'. *Dimorphodon* had a big beak-like mouth, probably for snapping up bugs, and wings about 150 centimetres across.

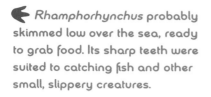
Rhamphorhynchus probably skimmed low over the sea, ready to grab food. Its sharp teeth were suited to catching fish and other small, slippery creatures.

Long wings

The Jurassic pterosaur *Rhamphorhynchus* (ram-FOE-rink-us) had wings slightly longer than your arms. It also had a long tail to help it steer in the air. Later pterosaurs lacked this tail. Some had a bony crest on the back of the head, which may have been colourful and was probably for display.

This fossil of the pterosaur *Pterodactylus* (ter-owe-DACK-till-us) shows its very long fourth finger bone, which supported the front of the wing, pointing down on the far right.

Back to the Jurassic

Across
1 This Jurassic pterosaur swooped low over the ocean to catch sea creatures

Down
1 On the end of a pterosaur's toe is a . . .
2 On the end of a pterosaur's leg is its . . .
3 A pterosaur's wing claws are on its . . .
4 A pterosaur flew by flapping its . . .
5 Some pterosaurs often caught slippery, scaly . . .
6 A pterosaur's wings were made of thin . . .

When did they live?

The Age of the Dinosaur lasted for more than 160 million years, from small meat-eaters like *Herrerasaurus* 228 million years ago, to the last big killer *Tyrannosaurus* 65 million years ago. But how do we know these dates and times?

Dating fossils

Some kinds of creatures, like ammonites, changed gradually over time and left many fossils. We can work out which creatures lived when from the ages of the rocks that the fossils are found in. If a dinosaur fossil is in the same age of rock as an ammonite fossil in a similar rock, and we know the approximate age of the ammonite, then we know the approximate age of the dinosaur.

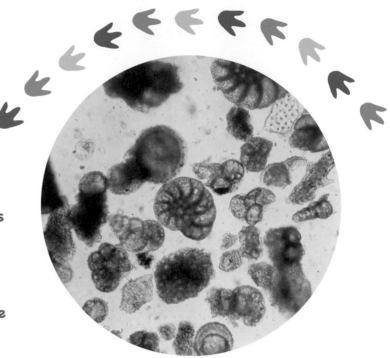

Fossils of tiny animals called foraminifera (forams), seen here under a microscope, are used to date other fossils found with them. Forams have lived in the sea for over 500 million years.

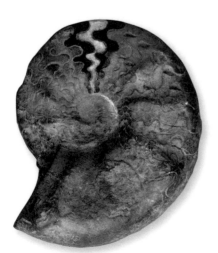  

Different kinds of ammonites lived at different times. The patterns on a Triassic ammonite (left) are simpler than on a Jurassic ammonite (middle). The knobbles on the last ammonite help to identify it as living in the Cretaceous. All this helps us to work out the age of other fossils found in similar rocks.

Who lived when?

Put these dinosaurs in order of when they lived, from oldest (1) to most recent (6)`.

Coelophysis ☐

Gallimimus ☐

Iguanodon ☐

Tyrannosaurus ☐

Microraptor ☐

Stegosaurus ☐

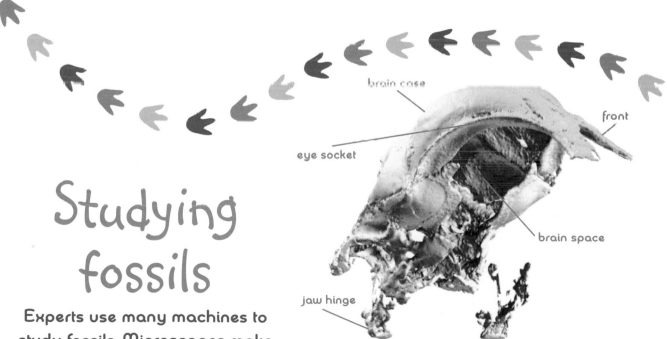

Studying fossils

Experts use many machines to study fossils. Microscopes make tiny details look huge. Laser scanners measure every part exactly. CT scanners see hidden holes and marks inside the rock.

brain case

front

eye socket

brain space

jaw hinge

◀ A CT scan inside the fossil skull of the first known bird, *Archaeopteryx* shows a space. When this bird was alive, its brain was in the space. Its shape shows which brain parts were well developed for seeing, hearing, balance and co-ordinating flight muscles.

What did they eat?

We can see that in living creatures, the size of the mouth and the shape of the teeth are suited to certain kinds of food. Long sharp teeth are good for grabbing and tearing up animal prey. Wide flat-topped teeth are best for munching plants.

Dinosaur diets

Fossils show that dinosaurs had many different shapes of mouth and teeth, which give clues to the food they ate long ago. There are more clues from the tiny marks on the fossil teeth, seen under a microscope. The marks are due to wear from eating the same kind of food, such as very tough leaves or narrow stems.

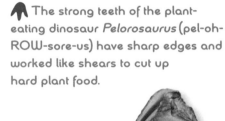

The strong teeth of the plant-eating dinosaur *Pelorosaurus* (pel-oh-ROW-sore-us) have sharp edges and worked like shears to cut up hard plant food.

Diplodocus (DI-plod-oh-kuss) had thin, straight, peg-like teeth that were no use for chewing hard plants. The teeth were like a rake to pull leaves off stems, which the dinosaur then swallowed for grinding up in its stomach.

Big and small teeth

The biggest dinosaur teeth belonged to the great meat-eaters. *Tyrannosaurus* had very strong teeth, as thick as big bananas and even longer, for enormous biting power. Duck-bill dinosaurs had the most teeth, with hundreds of them at the back of the jaws to chew the hardest plant foods like twigs and bark.

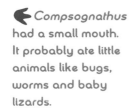
← *Compsognathus* had a small mouth. It probably ate little animals like bugs, worms and baby lizards.

Fossil droppings

Like all animals, dinosaurs got rid of food in their droppings, and these could form fossils! The fossil droppings are no longer squishy and smelly, because they are now made of rock. But they do contain many clues as to what dinosaurs ate.

Who ate what?

Draw lines between the dinosaurs and the food they ate.

← Fossil droppings, called coprolites, often have bits of leftover food in them. Seeds and bits of bark are from a plant-eater while a fish-eater's coprolites have fish bones and scales in them.

Halfway through

About 145 million years ago, halfway through the Age of the Dinosaur, the Jurassic Period ended and the Cretaceous Period began. The world was cooler and drier, with different living conditions for plants and animals.

➤ *Muttaburrasaurus* (MUT-a-BURR-a-SORE-us) was a plant-eating dinosaur in Australia during the Early Cretaceous.

Flowers

The Cretaceous saw new kinds of plants – those with flowers. Some were similar to today's water-lilies and magnolias. They were a new kind of food, so new animals evolved to eat them, including new kinds of dinosaurs.

🐾 Flowers like these magnolias are soft and delicate and fall apart, so fossils of them are very rare. The leaves however are more robust and fossils of leaf impressions can be found in rock.

Bigger than big

Sauropod dinosaurs in the Late Jurassic, such as *Brachiosaurus*, were huge. But during the Cretaceous some plant-eaters were even more gigantic. *Argentinosaurus* (AR-gent-eeno-sore-us) is known from only a few fossils in South America. They show it was probably almost 30 metres long and weighed over 60 tonnes.

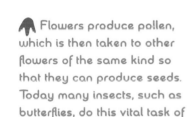 As different types of flowers appeared, animals such as beetles and early relatives of bees appeared too, and they pollinated the flowers.

Everything evolving

Flowers produce pollen, which is then taken to other flowers of the same kind so that they can produce seeds. Today many insects, such as butterflies, do this vital task of carrying the pollen.

As the animals changed to eat the new plants such as flowers, so these plants continued to evolve even more, for example, developing spines or a horrible taste to avoid being eaten. This shows how animals and plants all depend on each other and evolve together.

Together or alone?

Some plant-eating animals today live in great herds, like zebras or bison. Others stay mainly on their own, such as rhinos or moose. Fossils can help us to work out which dinosaurs were herd-dwellers and which probably lived by themselves.

Herds of *Iguanodon* probably trotted from one feeding place to another. Big adults protected the youngsters.

Ouranosaurus (oo-RAH-noh-sore-us) was a cousin of *Iguanodon*, with a tall sail-like hump on its back. Tall bones along the back supported the sail. It might have acted as a heating and cooling 'radiator'.

Lots of fossils

One of the main dinosaurs during the Early Cretaceous, 125 million years ago, was *Iguanodon*. Fossil-hunters have found remains from hundreds of these big plant-eaters in several places around the world.

Safety in numbers

Fossils of many *Iguanodon* were found jumbled together in one place. Maybe a group or herd of them lived together, helping each other to fight off enemies. Then they died together too, perhaps drowned in a sudden flood.

Humps and plates

1 Why do experts think that *Ouranosaurus* had a big hump on its back?

A To make it look bigger to enemies.
B To regulate its body temperature.
C To make rolling over more comfortable.

2 Why did armoured dinosaurs have strong protective plates and lumps in their skin?

A To protect against falling rocks.
B To stop their skin wearing away.
C To defend themselves against the teeth and claws of meat-eaters.

Lonely life

Armoured dinosaurs, or ankylosaurs, were also Cretaceous plant-eaters, but very different from *Iguanodon*. In each fossil find there is usually just one of them, so probably they lived alone. But they had big pieces or plates of bone over their body to protect against enemies.

◄ This fossil nodule would have been part of the thick, bony back of a dinosaur such as *Evoplocephalus* (you-OH-plo-kef-ah-luss). The ridge would have provided protection to the dinosaur.

► Armoured *Evoplocephalus* had a massive bony lump on its tail. It used this as a club that it could swing and hit its enemies with.

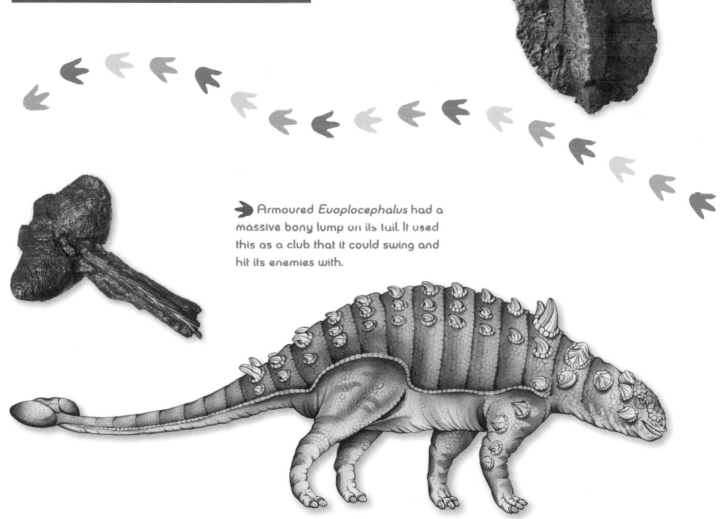

Duck-bills galore

Towards the end of the Age of the Dinosaur, it may have been very noisy. Strange honking and trumpet-like sounds echoed through the forests and swamps. It's those duck-bill dinosaurs again!

Many duck-bill fossils found in one place show that these dinosaurs probably lived in huge groups or herds.. The duck-bill *Maiasaura* (my-ah-SORE-ah) may have brought food to its babies in their nest.

Duck beak

The Late Cretaceous duck-bills, also called hadrosaurs, are named after the shape of their mouth. At the front this was wide and flat with no teeth, like a duck's beak or bill The back of the mouth had hundreds of strong teeth for chewing tough plant food.

Different duck-bills had different shaped crests. The largest crest, on *Parasaurolophus* (pa-ra-saw-ROL-off-us), was as big as you!

⬅ The elephant makes a loud trumpet sound by blowing through its trunk. Did duck-bills blow through the air passages (shown here in red) in their bony skull crests to make similar sounds?

Many duck-billed dinosaurs had odd bony shapes on their head, known as crests. Some crests were hollow and linked to the breathing tubes. As air blew through the crest, it may have made a loud noise. This could scare away enemies, or attract a mate, or gather herd members together.

Duck-bill dinosaurs like *Corythosaurus* (koh-rith-OH-sore-us) had a crest like a flat wedge. Individuals of the same species could recognise each other as they had the same shaped crest.

Built for speed

Most people know that the ostrich is a very fast runner. Late in Cretaceous times there were dinosaurs with a very similar body shape to the ostrich. These were called – guess – ostrich-dinosaurs!

 Gallimimus (gal-lee-MEEM-us) was one of the biggest ostrich-dinosaurs, taller than a person and longer than a car.

Long legs

The long legs of ostrich-dinosaurs let them take huge steps or strides. The strong muscles to move the legs were in the hips. The head, neck and arms were slim and light, to save weight for faster running.

 The ostrich can run almost twice as fast as a person. Maybe ostrich-dinosaurs were even faster!

Fastest of their kind

Fill in the missing letters to make the names of the fastest animals in their group.

Dinosaur G a _ _ i m _ m _ s

Mammal C h _ _ t _ h

Bird P _ r _ g r _ n _ f _ l c _ n

Fish S _ _ l f _ s h

Snake B l _ c k m _ m b _

Insect runner C _ c k r _ _ c h

Insect flier D r _ g _ n f l y

Giant claws

One of the great dinosaur mysteries is the fossil of a massive arm and hand with very long claws. The dinosaur they belonged to was called *Deinocheirus* (DINE-oh-KIRE-us). It may have been a huge ostrich-dinosaur over 10 metres long. But there are not enough fossils to be sure.

➤ The huge fossil arm and hand of *Deinocheirus* is taller than a person. Apart from this, no other fossils are known from this dinosaur.

No teeth

Ostrich-dinosaurs were like the ostrich in another way. They had no teeth. The mouth was a long strong beak, like a bird's. These dinosaurs probably ate any food they could find, such as leaves, seeds, fruits, buds and small animals like lizards and mammals.

➤ *Deinocheirus* could have looked like this. It might have been as big as *Tyrannosaurus*, with a covering of fluffy feathers!

A dry place

During Cretaceous times, some parts of the world became quite dry. Fossils show that plants were small and tough, like those in semi-deserts today. Dinosaurs and other animals may have lived in conditions with dry and rainy seasons but hot all year round.

In the Gobi Desert fossil-hunters use many tools, including shovels, pick-axes and hammers, to uncover their finds. The hot sun and dust storms make work very difficult.

Tough times

In East Asia about 75 million years ago there were dinosaurs such as *Protoceratops* (pro-toe-KER-ah-tops) and *Velociraptor* (vel-OSS-ee-rap-tor). Today this area is the Gobi Desert, and it is even more dry and dusty. Plants struggle to grow and animals walk many miles to find water.

The skull of *Protoceratops* has no teeth at the front, but a sharp-edged beak to cut off bits of plants. The rear of the mouth has strong teeth for cutting, like scissors.

Neck frill

Protoceratops was a type of dinosaur called a ceratopsian. This group had a sharp beak at the front of the mouth and a bony frill around the neck, like a tall collar. Some had lumps or sharp horns on the nose.

🦶 Here you can see the fossil skull of an adult *Psittacosaurus* with many skeletons of babies around it. This dinosaur may have looked after the babies of others of its kind, like a nursery.

🦶 The skull of *Psittacosaurus* had a very strong, parrot-like beak at the front. This dinosaur was one of the early ceratopsians, living over 100 million years ago.

Parrot-beak

Psittacosaurus (SIT-ak-oh-sore-us) was one of the first ceratopsians, but quite small at about 2 metres long and 1 metre tall. It did not have a large neck frill like later ceratopsians such as *Triceratops*.

🦶 One of the last and biggest ceratopsians was *Triceratops* (tri-KER-ah-tops), more than 8 metres long. It lived in North America. It may have used its horns in defence against predators such as *Tyrannosaurus*.

Raptors rule!

Some of the most fearsome of all dinosaurs lived during Cretaceous times. They were not huge hunters like *Tyrannosaurus*. They were smaller – and probably sneakier. They are called 'raptor' dinosaurs or dromaeosaurs.

Oviraptor (OH-vee-RAP-tor) was similar to the main group of raptors, but it had a bird-like beak and no teeth.

Deadly killers

Raptors were certainly meat-eaters. They stood up and ran on their back legs. They had sharp teeth, big eyes, and a big brain for their body size, so they could have been quite clever. They also had a deadly sharp, curved claw on each foot. Many of them had feathers.

The North American raptor *Deinonychus* (die-NON-i-kuss) was over 3 metres long. It may have hunted in a group or pack as shown here attacking a *Tenontosaurus* (ten-ON-toe-sore-us).

Like most raptors, *Sinornithosaurus* (sine-OR-nith-oh-SORE-us) had claws on its hands and feet. It was about 2 metres long and lived in what is now China.

The raptor's big curved claw, on the second toe, could slash and slice enemies and victims.

Big and small

The biggest raptor was *Utahraptor* (YOO-tah-RAP-tor) from North America, seven metres long and as heavy as a grizzly bear. Tiny *Microraptor* from China was just 50 centimetres in length.

Velociraptor was probably about as big as you – but was much more fierce!

Small to big

Put these raptor dinosaurs in order of size, smallest (1) to largest (4).

Deinonychus ☐
Utahraptor ☐
Velociraptor ☐
Microraptor ☐

T. rex or T. bataar?

Everyone has heard of *Tyrannosaurus rex* (T. rex). But do you know about *Tarbosaurus bataar* (TAR-bow-SORE-us bat-ARE)? These two deadly giants were almost the same size, and the same shape, and lived at the same time – the end of the Age of the Dinosaur.

⬅ At the time of *Tarbosaurus* and *Tyrannosaurus*, about 70 to 65 million years ago, the world's continents were drifting farther apart. You can see the shapes we know today, but closer together.

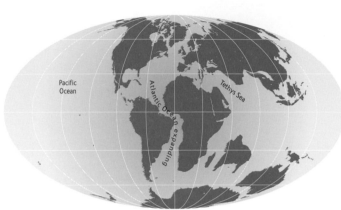

Pacific Ocean

Atlantic Ocean expanding

Tethys Sea

➡ *Tarbosaurus* was perhaps slightly smaller than *Tyrannosaurus* (opposite), but otherwise very similar. Did it and *Tyrannosaurus* run after prey? Probably, but not as fast as most people think.

The two Ts

Tyrannosaurus lived in North America. Tarbosaurus was from East Asia. They were both massive meat-eaters over 10 metres long and five tonnes in weight. They had a huge mouth full of sharp, curved teeth. Their back legs were big and powerful, yet their arms were tiny and probably useless.

Over 30 specimens of Tyrannosaurus fossils are known, some with almost all the bones and teeth. Tyrannosaurus and Tarbosaurus teeth curved backwards to stop victims escaping from their bite.

Same or different?

Were Tyrannosaurus and Tarbosaurus really the same kind of dinosaur? Some experts think so, and they say that all Tarbosaurus fossils should be called Tyrannosaurus. Other experts say they need to find and study more fossils to be sure.

The end of the age

Just over 65 million years ago, life changed. Exactly what happened is not clear. But the results are very clear. All the dinosaurs of the time died out. The Cretaceous Period ended, and with it, the Age of the Dinosaur.

Mass extinctions?

When many kinds of living things die out at the same time, it is a mass extinction. This happened at the end of the Cretaceous. Probably a giant rock from space, an asteroid, smashed into the Earth. It set off earthquakes, volcanoes and huge tsunami waves. The asteroid impact threw dust into the air that blotted out the sun.

Quetzalcoatlus was one of the last pterosaurs. It was also one of the biggest, with wings more than 10 metres across.

One day a strange glow appeared in the sky. It was an asteroid from space heading to Earth – the beginning of the end.

As plants died after the asteroid strike, dinosaurs like *Triceratops* had no food and so they perished. Meat-eaters that preyed on them, like *Tyrannosaurus*, also starved.

Disaster

Plants could not grow. Animals were cold and hungry and began to die. Apart from dinosaurs, flying pterosaurs also died out. So did sea creatures such as plesiosaurs, mosasaurs and ammonites. Many smaller creatures, and lots of plants too, disappeared forever.

Word search

Find six words linked to the great disaster that finished the Age of Dinosaurs.

```
S U N F D A T
K P M E N D S
Z L A O Y T U
G T L C O L D
H R U V E A G
```

Ferns are one of the first plants to grow back after mass extinctions and fern fossils are very common in the rocks after the end of the Cretaceous.

What didn't die out

The mass extinction that ended the Age of the Dinosaur killed off millions of animals and plants. But some types survived. They continued, and evolved, and their kind are still living today.

Following the Age of the Dinosaur new kinds of plants and animals spread across the land. Different flowers and trees appeared with new kinds of mammals and birds living among them.

The coelacanth fishes were thought to be extinct for 80 million years, since the Age of the Dinosaur finished. Then a living one was caught less than 100 years ago and more have been discovered since.

Who survived?

Animal survivors include birds and flying insects like dragonflies. On land there were mammals, reptiles such as lizards and snakes, and small creatures such as bugs, spiders and worms. In the water there were crocodiles, turtles, frogs, sharks, starfish and various kinds of shellfish. Many plants survived too, such as mosses, ferns, conifer trees and various kinds of flowers.

Living fossils

Some living things today are very similar to their relatives from the Age of the Dinosaur, although not exactly the same. They are known as 'living fossils'. The way they behave, feed and breed helps us to work out what life was like during dinosaur times.

The nautilus of the deep sea today has changed little from its relations of 450 million years ago.

The tuatara of New Zealand looks like a lizard. But it is a different type of reptile, with relatives going back even before dinosaurs.

Today's great white shark is a puny weakling compared to its extinct cousin *Carcharodon megalodon* (car-cha-ROW-don mega-LOW-don), which was three times longer!

Studying fossil teeth from *C. megalodon* shows that it died out around one and a half million years ago. Its teeth were many times bigger than the teeth of the great white shark.

Sneaky peek to the future

After the Age of the Dinosaur, evolution carried on. New kinds of mammals, birds, reptiles, fish, insects, worms and other animals were joined by new types of flowers and trees. Evolution continues today and will continue into the future.

Our own kind, or species, is called *Homo sapiens* (hoe-mow SAP-ee-ens). Our evolution has been very fast, from living in caves and using stone tools to changing the face of the planet with cities, roads and industries in less than 20,000 years.

A changing world

Our world changes faster than ever. We face problems such as global warming, pollution and using too much energy. Every day, more people take over more wild places. Animals and plants face huge threats and many are becoming extinct.

Rats are great pests – because they are a success of modern evolution. Their success relies on us. Rats live near humans and eat all kinds of food that we grow, store or throw away.

What will survive?

Which of these animals do you think will survive into the future, and which are in danger of dying out?

Polar bear ☐
Fox ☐
Cockroach ☐
Siberian tiger ☐
Californian condor bird ☐
Housefly ☐
Rhino ☐
Seagull ☐

← Animals and plants that die today may leave fossils for the future. Who will dig them up to study them?

Future world

Dinosaurs ruled for 160 million years. Our own kind, modern humans, have been around for a thousand times less. Fossils show that a mammal-type animal like us usually lasts from two to five million years. How will humans do? Which new kinds of weird and wonderful creatures will evolve in millions of years to come?

New kinds of weird and wonderful creatures!

Draw your animal of the future in the space below and give it a name. Where does it live — in the sea, the land or the sky? Does it have claws or protective plates? Does it have horns or wings?

Answers

How well did you do on the activities?

 07 Word search

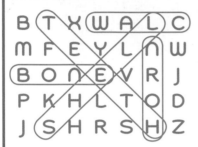

 11 Were they alive then?

Starfish, sea-lilies, ammonites, sharks

 15 Which is which?

crocodile

dolphin

shark

icthyosaur

 21 Back to the Jurassic

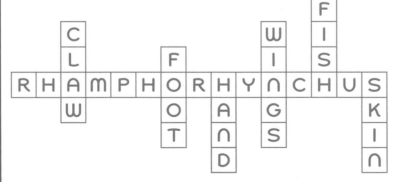

 23 Who lived when?

Coelophysis [1]   Gallimimus [5]   Iguanodon [3]   Tyrannosaurus [6]

Microraptor [4]   Stegasaurus [2]

Who ate what?

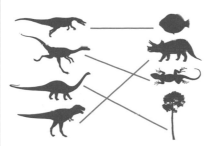

Humps and plates
Question 1 = B   Question 2 = C

Fastest of their kind

Dinosaur - Gallimimus   Fish – Sailfish
Mammal - Cheetah   Snake – Black mamba
Bird - Peregrine falcon   Insect runner – Cockroach
                                 Insect flier – Dragonfly

Small to big

Deinonychus [3]   Utahraptor [4]   Velociraptor [2]   Microraptor [1]

Word search

What will survive?
Survive – fox, cockroach, housefly, seagull
At risk of dying out – polar bear, Siberian tiger, Californian condor bird, rhino

About the Natural History Museum...

The Natural History Museum in South Kensington, London has a collection of over 70 million specimens from meteorites and dinosaurs to plants and hippos, some of which you can see in the amazing exhibitions in our galleries.

Our most exciting exhibition for people like you who are interested in dinosaurs is our Dinosaurs exhibition. Here you can see small feathered dinosaurs and huge plant-eating dinosaurs and the fearsome *T. rex*. And don't forget to say hello to Dippy our welcoming *Diplodocus* in the Central Hall

Go to our website to find activities, games and a directory full of facts on every dinosaur we know about, as well as lots of pictures. www.nhm.ac.uk/kids-only/dinosaurs/

Read our exciting books about dinosaurs
Dinosaurs: A Thrilling Journey through Prehistoric Times
Dinosaur Hunters
Dippy: The Tale of a Museum Icon
Kid's Only
The Natural History Museum Book of Dinosaurs
Natural History Museum Dinosaur Sticker Book
Natural History Museum Dot-to-Dot

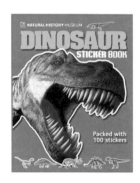

Available through the Museum bookshop online and every good bookshop.
www.nhm.ac.uk/business-centre/publishing/books/dinosaurs/index.html

First published by the Natural History Museum,
Cromwell Road, London SW7 5BD
© The Trustees of the Natural History Museum, London 2011.
All Rights Reserved.

This edition © The Trustees of the Natural History Museum,
London 2014. All Rights Reserved.

10 9 8 7 6 5 4 3 2 1

ISBN 978 0 565 09329 7

Designed by Mercer Design, London
Reproduction by Saxon Digital Services
Printed by Toppan Leefung Printing Limited

Front cover: Dinosaur © NHMPL; Sky © hide-mori/amana images/Getty Images; Landscape © Benjamin G. Randle/Flickr/
Getty Images Picture Credits: p.3 top, middle © John Sibbick/NHMPL, p.3 bottom © Roger Harris/Science Photo Library; p.4
top © Michael Long/NHMPL, p.4 middle © Jaime Chirinos/Science Photo Library; p.5 top © Tim White/NHMPL; p.7 top © Paul
Barrett; p.8 bottom © Lawrence Freytag/Istockphoto; p.9 top © De Agostini/NHMPL; p.9 bottom © Anness Publishing/NHMPL;
p.10 bottom © Charles G. Messing, Nova Southeastern University; p.10 bottom left © Graham Cripps/NHMPL; p.12 top ©
Anness Publishing/NHMPL; p.12 bottom © Roger Harris/Science Photo Library; p.13 top © Sue Scott; p.14 bottom © Graham
Cripps/NHMPL; p.15 top © Richard Bizley/Science Photo Library; p.16 © Roger Harris/Science Photo Library; p.17 top © De
Agostini/NHMPL; p.18 top © John Sibbick/NHMPL, p.18 middle © Christian Darkin/Science Photo Library; p.19 top © John
Sibbick/NHMPL; p.20 top © De Agostini/NHMPL; p.25 top © Walter Myers/Science Photo Library; p.26 top © John Sibbick/
NHMPL, p.26 middle © Pavlo Maydikov; p.27 bottom © James Mojonnier; p.28 top © John Sibbick/NHMPL, p.28 bottom © De
Agostini/NHMPL; p.30 top © John Sibbick/NHMPL, p.35 middle © Rick Seargeant, p.31 bottom © De Agostini/NHMPL; p.32
bottom © John Carnemolla; p.33 bottom © Anness Publishing/NHMPL; p.34 top © Louie Psihoyos/Science Faction/Corbis;
p.34 bottom right © John Cancalosi / ardea.com; p.36 top © Kokoro/NHMPL, p.36 bottom © John Sibbick/NHMPL, p.37 top ©
Geological Museum of China/NHMPL; p.38 bottom © Friedrich Saurer/Science Photo Library; p.40 top © John Sibbick/NHMPL;
bottom © Mark Garlick/Science Photo Library; p.41 top © Mauricio Anton/Science Photo Library; p.42 bottom © Peter
Scoones/Science Photo Library; p.43 middle © Norma Cornes; p.43 bottom right © Stephen Sweet; p.44 top © John Sibbick/
NHMPL; bottom © Oleg Kozlov; p.45 top © Claudio Arnese.